D0620103

THE BOOK OF
NAME
SIGNS

NAMING IN AMERICAN SIGN LANGUAGE

SAMUEL J. SUPALLA

DawnSignPress

SAN DIEGO, CA.

Production by *Tina Jo Breindel, Joe Dannis, Iosep MacDougall*
Edited by *Marla Hatrak, Robin Supalla*
Sign Illustrations by *Paul Setzer*

Sign Models:

Sandra Ammons

Tina Jo Breindel

Bob Hiltermann

Iosep MacDougall

Sam Supalla

Front Cover Photograph: *American School for the Deaf*

Printed in the United States of America

ISBN: 0-915035-30-8

Library of Congress Catalog Card Number: 92-072696

10 9 8 7 6 5 4 3 2 1

Quantity discounts for schools and bookstores are available.
For more information, contact:

DawnSignPress
9080 Activity Road, Suite A
San Diego, CA 92126-4421
(619)549-5330 V/TDD

For my brother, Ted

CONTENTS

FOREWORD ix

PREFACE xi

INTRODUCTION xiii

PART ONE NAME SIGNS 1
CHAPTER ONE MY NAME SIGN STORY 3
CHAPTER TWO HOW TO FORM A NAME SIGN 7
CHAPTER THREE HOW TO USE A NAME SIGN 15
CHAPTER FOUR ORIGINS OF NAME SIGNS 21
ENDNOTES 37

PART TWO THE NAME SIGN LIST 41
CHOOSING A NAME SIGN 42

A 44
B 46
C 48
D 50
E 52
F 54
G 56
H 58
I 60
J 63
K 64

L 66

M 68

N 72

O 74

P 76

Q 79

R 80

S 82

T 84

U 86

V 88

W 90

X 92

Y 94

LIST OF REFERENCES 97

ABOUT THE AUTHOR 99

FOREWORD

THIS BOOK IS ABOUT NAMES in American Sign Language. American Deaf people have two sets of names, one in English and the other in American Sign Language (ASL). Typically at first introductions, Deaf people exchange their first and last English names through the use of "fingerspelling," or executing a handshape for each letter of the name. The subject of this book is the other set of names, popularly called "name signs." Good name signs must suit a number of requirements, many of which have never been explained in any detail until this book.

Name signs are a linguist's dream. There are only a small number of possible name forms, compared to the much larger number of possible forms of all other ASL signs. Name signs are formed by combining one of a small set of possible hand configurations with certain possible locations, which are then blended with a limited number of movements. Sam Supalla was the first among us to see that name signs offered a clever way to probe into the complicated rule of how pieces of signs are combined to make true ASL signs. By looking at name signs – a more manageable set of signs, we have a good picture of what the rest of ASL signs must look like.

This alone would make a book about name signs worthwhile, but Sam has taken the story further into interesting terrain: the link between language and culture. What a purely linguistic analysis of name signs would leave out is the fact that name signs not only name Deaf people, but signify them. In this way, name signs reveal much about the cultural lives of Deaf people. Name signs signify who is related to whom, also who is more powerful, or more important. Name signs track relationships within families, groups, and communities of Deaf people and the hearing people they live with. Deaf families share similar name signs. Professors teaching the same subject are given similar name signs. Certain types of name signs are reserved for the more powerful members of a community. Name signs can be like a map, tracking a community "tree" of relationships.

The key to tracking this web of relationships is to understand the different types of name signs and what they signify. As Sam explains, there are two major types of name signs in ASL. Arbitrary name signs, traditional among Deaf people, require the use of an alphabetic handshape drawn from the fingerspelled inventory of handshapes. Descriptive name signs are favored less; they ignore the alphabetic convention. Instead, they use representations of some personal or physical feature of the person named. Arbitrary name signs are thought to be "traditional," "correct," and "grown up," and descriptive name signs, "childish." Deaf children often invent descriptive name signs for each other, but they are expected to replace them when they grow older for more acceptable name signs.

Significantly, the last twenty or thirty years, a new type of name sign has emerged. Neither fully arbitrary nor fully descriptive, this new type of name sign is a curious mixture of the two. Sam explains that the new name signs take fingerspelled handshapes but combine them with movements found in descriptive name signs. Why this peculiar combination? Why in the last twenty or thirty years? For one thing, the emergence of these signs coincides with the appearance of new "visitors" to the community of Deaf people: adults who learn ASL as a second language. Curiously, instead of adopting arbitrary name signs as Deaf people do, these "visitors" use a different, newly created type of name sign. Why? I will let Sam tell the story. It is one of the more interesting I have read about cultural change in the community of Deaf people.

This book will please those of us who like "how-to" books, but the gift of the book is that it is "how-to" at two levels: linguistic and cultural. Name signs are structurally "real" signs; they must co-exist with other signs of the language. But name signs also signify relationships: together and apart, same and different, expected and unusual. They show the links and ties that bind us together and remind us that, in the midst of language, there is identity and place.

Carol A. Padden
University of California, San Diego

PREFACE

THIS BOOK IS ABOUT NAME SIGNS, a very personal aspect of American Sign Language which is worthy of special attention. Name signs in American Sign Language (ASL) first received my attention ten years ago when I was working as a research assistant at the Salk Institute in La Jolla, California with Ursula Bellugi. It was there that I became fascinated with name signs and was able to publish a paper focusing on the linguistic description of ASL name signs. Only recently has more research work appeared and been published on name signs; they have helped make this book possible. I am grateful that we are finally able to not only use name signs, but to understand and appreciate their role in ASL.

This book is unique as it provides a description of as well as a reference for ASL name signs. My basic motivation in writing this book lies in my attempts to preserve traditional name signs for future generations of Deaf people. I owe many thanks to Ben Bahan and Joe Dannis, both of DawnSignPress, who provided me with the support I needed to implement this book. Tina Wix's help was also greatly appreciated. She spent an entire summer organizing the name sign list and photographing hundreds of name signs. Many thanks to Sandra Ammons, Tina Jo Breindel, Bob Hiltermann, and Iosep MacDougall, the sign models, as well as the illustrator, Paul Setzer; and to my wife, Robin, who undertook the dreaded job of text copyediting. Loy Golladay, Michael Olson, Clayton Valli, Carol Padden, and Gil Eastman were extremely helpful in filling in gaps historical facts regarding name signs. Carol Padden and Jeffrey Davis provided invaluable comments on earlier drafts of this book. I thank all of these people for their support and belief in me.

Last, I want to pay special tribute to my mentors who taught me how to conduct research on name signs: Ursula Bellugi and Ted Supalla. *The Book of Name Signs* is dedicated to my brother, Ted, for helping my distraught parents by creating my name sign, thus passing on the tradition of name signs to me and future generations.

Samuel J. Supalla
Tucson, Arizona
June 3, 1992

INTRODUCTION

NAMES AND NAMING are one of those things that many of us take for granted. Although there has been extensive research on naming done over the years, there are still many theoretical questions left unanswered. Could a person function without a name? What would it feel like to be a nameless person? Could a town function if all its citizens had no names? How could a barber talk to his customers if he could not make reference to another person? Certainly, their conversations would be limited!

It appears that names and naming are essential for the socialization of a person in a community. Naming of people is found in all cultures of the world. In the United States, a birth certificate is a testimony to the importance of a proper name. In most bookstores, an entire shelf is found reserved for books on naming babies. These books include long lists of possible names from which people may choose. It seems obvious that no one is expected to give a baby the name, "Flour." Nor is one expected to invent a proper name such as "Caprula." In both instances, these names would be considered deviant from the tradition and considered exceptions. On the other hand, "Jeanette" may be a traditional proper name, but it would not be used to name a boy. There are many "rules" based on tradition for naming people, and name books serve as a reference and/or guide to help people with this process.

Proper names make up a complex system of formation and use. More importantly, in each culture throughout the world, there may be a distinct system for forming and using proper names. The American Sign Language (ASL) Name Sign System is one system that has served Deaf people for a long time. Although most Deaf people have a

(English) name printed on their birth certificate, they need another form (other than vocal) to express their name sign in daily life. A name sign is most effective in serving as a symbol for the identity of a Deaf person, and it has helped to make socialization within the Deaf community possible.

Historically, name signs have been used only among Deaf people, although this has changed as more and more hearing people are learning ASL as a second or foreign language. Unfortunately, too many novice signers possess name signs that are non-traditional in nature, similar to "Flour" or "Caprula" as discussed above. More distressing is the rising number of deaf children being given non-traditional name signs. Novice signers are also often unaware of the rules for creating name signs as well as the pragmatic functions of name sign use. For example, hearing people typically vocalize a person's name when trying to get his/her attention. This behavior is often generalized by novice signers when they sign "Hey, Bob" to get a person's attention. Traditionally, a name sign would not be used in this manner. Thus, a basic question remains, "What constitutes traditional form and use of name signs?"

In order to understand ASL name sign system in general, several misconceptions must be cleared up. Many people, particularly those just learning the language, believe that name signs have an inherent meaning and often demand this meaning when they encounter a name sign. One might ask, "What does your name sign mean?" or "Why is that your name sign?" Imagine the same question being asked of someone's spoken name. Though not unimaginable, one would rarely ask, "Why is your name 'Bill'?" or "What does 'Jeanette' mean?" Most traditional name signs do not have any inherent meaning.

The goal of *The Book of Name Signs* is to help readers understand, create, and use name signs according to the tradition and to appreciate them as an integral part of the language and culture of the Deaf community. This book was made possible by formal research conducted on name signs by many people including myself. My own research serves as the basis for this book, which is divided into two parts. The first part discusses name signs in general, and the second part includes a list of over 500 name signs. After much thought, I have decided that an ideal introduction to ASL name signs would be to tell you how I received my own name sign. You may wonder what my name sign looks like and how I give others name signs. The following story will serve as a starting point as well through the world of name signs.

THE BOOK OF
NAME SIGNS

NAMING IN AMERICAN SIGN LANGUAGE

PART ONE
NAME
SIGNS

MY NAME SIGN STORY

T O MY PARENTS' SURPRISE, I was a boy, thus bringing our family total to four sons. I was the fourth and last child. While my mother lay in bed exhausted, my father was frantic because he had picked out a name only for a girl, not a boy. The nurse was pushy and kept asking my father for my name. On my birth certificate, my father wrote: Samuel James Supalla. When my father entered the recovery room, he assured my mother that everything was taken care of, including my new name. My mother was surprised and asked for my name, and my father fingerspelled it out. Fortunately, my mother liked it, but she soon became frantic when she began to think of a name sign for me. The crisis had set in; my father had made a big mistake! Since my oldest brother's name was Steve, the /S/ handshape was already reserved for his name sign. We would end up having identical name signs!

It was my mother's preference to have a name sign on the chin, using the handshape for the initial of the first name for each of her children. Steve has the /S/ handshape with its side touching the chin location twice. My second and third brothers, Ted and David, have /T/ and /D/ handshapes touching the same location. The idea behind having the chin location for all of my brothers' name signs represents family unity. If I had a name beginning with /S/, then my name sign would have to be outside the "family location." My mother was upset; I would not be part of the family! My father stood there dumbfounded.

I was nameless as far as name signs are concerned for three long weeks. It was my brother, Ted, at six years old, who helped create my name sign. He arrived home by train for Christmas from the Washington School for the Deaf in Vancouver. When he saw me for the first time, he asked my mother for my name sign. She responded sadly by saying there was none and explained the whole story. Ted quickly came up with a name sign. My mother took it as a blessing. It is still the /S/ handshape, but it moves from one side of the chin to the other. The family location is still preserved, and the name sign is appropriate as well. Thus, I really think of myself as being born around December 23rd, with the help of my brother, Ted!

Similar to Ted, I found myself assigning name signs at the age of six. By then, my father had quit the farming business, and we were living in a small town in Oregon. I was enrolled in the Oregon School for the Deaf in Salem. There, I encountered many children my own age, most without name signs. I was surprised to learn that their parents were hearing and not able to sign. My brother, Steve, was the only hearing member in my family, but he could sign. I remember clearly the chaos when I tried to refer to one of my peers in any conversation. I had to literally point to the person when I was trying to talk about him. I would be lucky if he was close by. Because I was a native signer, I was given the privilege of assigning name signs to my peers. I remember one boy coming up to me while I was skateboarding. He had yet to master my language, but I could understand his request. He wanted his own name sign, and I gave him one; his face gleamed with joy.

My story of growing up with name signs contains some interesting patterns. First, my name sign has some kind of reference to my written (English) name with the /S/ handshape. Second, the chin location of my name sign incorporates the notion of family unity. Third, most deaf children are assigned a name sign by each other, and not by their parents. Most important is that my name sign is part of a long history extending back to the founding of the first permanent school for the deaf in the United States.

My name sign story seems to be a continuing saga as I have also been given another name sign by Deaf people living outside the United States. In becoming acquainted with two Deaf Frenchmen who were visiting this country, I was astonished to see that my name sign was not "fitting" to them. I remember clearly how they responded blankly when I demonstrated my name sign to them. They turned to each other, signing in French Sign Language, and decided on their own "French" name sign for me. It was a representation of my "pointed nose." One of the Deaf Frenchmen explained that this would be the name sign used to refer to me back in France. This experience helps confirm the fact that name signs can vary greatly abroad.

In order to gain a more complete understanding of the American Name Sign System, we need to explore the formation of name signs, their uses, and their origins.

CHAPTER TWO

HOW TO FORM A NAME SIGN

IN THIS CHAPTER, the reader will gain an understanding of how name signs are formed according to tradition. There are two basic systems of name signs used in the United States: **descriptive** and **arbitrary**. Examples and illustrations of each type will be provided in this text.

The basic distinction between the two systems is whether or not a name sign has a meaning.[1] For example, my name sign, given to me at birth, has no meaning other than it represents the initial of my written (English) name. It does not indicate reference to my physical appearance or any personal characteristics. Although my name sign incorporates the concept of family unity, when one sees my name sign for the first time, this additional meaning cannot be detected. If my name sign was presented along with all of my brothers, then the family unity pattern of our name signs (i.e., sharing the same chin location) would be noticed. Thus my name sign is essentially arbitrary in nature, and it is part of the Arbitrary Name Sign (ANS) System. The following is an illustration of my name sign:

Author's Arbitrary Name Sign

The second ASL name sign system is based upon some personal characteristic and is called the Descriptive Name Sign (DNS) System. These name signs are made in accordance with the ASL rules which apply to all handshapes, movements, and locations used to describe a person's characteristics or behavior. The handshapes are classifiers used within the language to refer to sizes, shapes, objects, and people.[2] For example, a person with visible buck teeth may possess a DNS based on his or her most salient physical characteristic. In this case, the handshape would be based on the shape of the individual's teeth. The location would be on the mouth, and the movement would be repeated to indicate that the sign is a noun. The result is the DNS illustrated below:

Descriptive Name Sign: BUCKTEETH

This DNS example may be viewed as negative in nature; however, DNSes can be neutral, positive or negative. In one study, in which 450 ASL name signs were collected, only 86 or 19 percent were DNSes as opposed to 364 or 81 percent which were ANSes.[3] It appears that ANS is the dominant type of name sign found in the Deaf community. In addition, the ANS System is standardized and widely used across the country, although there are some exceptions.[4] At the Lexington School for the Deaf in New York City, deaf children's "name signs" were for many years assigned to correspond to their locker numbers.[5] For years, these students were known by their locker numbers. During a recent visit to the school, I found that the use of numbers for name signs is no longer promoted. However, the older alumni of the school reportedly still use their locker-number name signs, especially with each other.

There are important distinctions between an English proper name and an ASL name sign. Once an ANS or DNS is formed, it is strictly a one-word unit, unlike a full English name where three-word units prevail, the first, middle, and last names. Moreover, an ANS or DNS will not change its form into a diminutive (e.g., from Robert to Bob). My own written name is Samuel, but, when I was younger, I fingerspelled or wrote it as Sammy. Later, I changed it to Sam, which is what I currently use. Yet, for official occasions such as signatures, I write Samuel. In contrast, my name sign has remained the same through time and for all types of occasions.

My first name's written form, Sam, is fingerspelled according to the letters, S-A-M. Recall that my father fingerspelled my full name to my mother in the hospital. Fingerspelling written names does occur in the Deaf community; however, one needs to understand that the form of a fully fingerspelled name is not natural. A true ASL sign can possess a maximum of two handshapes but no more.[6] For S-A-M and most names, the handshape number exceeds two. Moreover, fingerspelled words are generally considered cumbersome and slow as compared to signs. For the reasons stated here, a fingerspelled name cannot function effectively as a sign. Therefore, name signs are used since naturalness is what distinguishes a name sign from that of a fingerspelled name.[7] In some cases, however, Deaf people do not have name signs. In these instances, names tend to be short (e.g., A-N-N) or contain letters that flow for fingerspelling (e.g., L-A-R-R-Y).[8]

My name sign falls into the category of the ANS System, which is most popular among Deaf people. In order to form an ANS, the handshape must be alphabetic to represent the initial of one's written first, middle, or last name. Mine is an /S/ representing the initial of my first name. Any of 25 alphabetical handshapes are acceptable.[9] Only the /Z/ handshape is not used.

There are three types of locations and movement available to form an ANS. The first type is the **ANS in Neutral Space** where the handshape is placed in the signing space in front of the signer. The second type is the **ANS with Single Location on Body** where the handshape is placed on a single location on the body and the movement for contact is repeated. The third type is the **ANS with Dual Locations on Body** where the handshape uses two locations on the body moving from one to another.[10] The following illustrations depict each ANS type using a /C/ handshape:

| Neutral Space | Single Location on Body | Dual Locations on Body |

My own name sign is an ANS with Dual Locations on Body with the /S/ handshape moving from one side of the chin to the other. Great care must be taken in how handshapes make contact with the body. For example, the handshape for my name sign makes its contact with the side of the hand and not the palm or the knuckles.[11] The list of ANSes in the second part of this book includes illustrations of each ANS for appropriate formation.

One popular misconception concerning ASL name signs is that they are all descriptive in nature. Novice signers often ask for the meaning behind a name sign. The fact is that most do not have any meaning beyond serving as a name sign, and most are ANSes. The increasing number of non-traditional name sign are often a result of mixing the two systems (DNS and ANS). Unfortunately, the increase of such name signs coincides with the dramatic increase in hearing people learning ASL as a second/foreign language. For example, one hearing person who learned ASL has the name sign as shown on the following page.

The handshape is an /S/ for the initial of the person's first (English) name, and it is located next to the eye. The movement is twisting the wrist up and down to indicate the movement of eyelids. The meaning is that this person characteristically winks a lot.[12] This name sign is not characteristic of either a DNS or ANS.

Non-traditional Name Sign

If the name sign is to be a traditional DNS, the handshape would not be a letter of the alphabet, but rather an ASL classifier. The appropriate classifier handshape would indicate the shape of the eyelids. If the same name sign is to be a traditional ANS, the location would not be at the eye, but would be formed at the nearest acceptable location, which is the temple. The following illustrations are the DNS and ANS alternatives to the above non-traditional name sign:

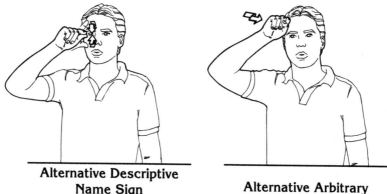

Alternative Descriptive Name Sign

Alternative Arbitrary

11

An important point to keep in mind is that the ANS and DNS Systems should be kept separate according to tradition. However, one should take note that there are many instances of "playing with name signs." In these cases, the motivation is to create humor with ASL and the manual alphabet, perhaps by combining a regular sign and an alphabetical handshape. This can be clearly illustrated with some of the name signs developed for famous people. For example, the name sign for former President Nixon is made by using an /N/ handshape with the sign LIE. Although the sign for LIE is produced with a /B/ handshape, in Nixon's name sign, the /B/ is replaced with that of an /N/ to represent the initial of the Nixon name. Using this combination, the meaning becomes "Nixon-the-liar." The following illustrations depict the original sign, LIE and the name sign for Nixon:

LIE   NIXON-THE-LIAR

According to my observations, the motivation for novice signers' non-traditional name signs is rather naive and based on their belief of what a name sign should look like. This misconception of how name signs are formed may be attributed to an incomplete understanding of the ASL Name Sign System and of Deaf culture.[13] According to the tradition, a non-traditional name sign can be accepted only if it is intended for amusement. Thus, if one possesses a non-traditional name sign and intends it to be serious, it would seem that this person is ignorant of name signs in general.

The number of hearing people now learning ASL as a second or foreign language requires our special attention. For example, in

California alone, there is an estimated 10,000 students taking ASL courses each year.[14] As far as name signs are concerned, I have observed an interesting pattern among hearing signers. They tend to not give themselves a name sign, but rather, they often insist on having a Deaf person assign them one. This may be considered appropriate; however, to make the matter more complex, the name sign assigned by the Deaf person is often non-traditional. This appears to be a paradox as one expects that Deaf signers would be assigning traditional name signs as they do each other and their own children. One possible explanation lies in the misconceptions on the part of novice signers as discussed earlier and that Deaf signers often try to accommodate them. There is another explanation that non-traditional name signs help to identify novice signers as "hearing" for Deaf signers.[15] This may imply that novice signers are not aware of the function behind possessing a non-traditional name sign. One way or another, non-traditional name signs appear to exist as a result of contact between the Deaf and hearing communities through signing.

Deaf people have responded unfavorably to the increase of non-traditional name signs within their community. According to one study, there is a concern expressed over this increase and a belief that hearing people are "taking over" the name sign system and molding it to their liking.[16] This concern is well-justified by the sheer number of hearing people possessing non-traditional name signs. This is coupled with the fact that most deaf children are born to hearing parents and often lack contact with the Deaf community (e.g., through mainstreaming) and its name sign system. If these current trends continue, the traditional distinction between the two name sign systems could become "blurred," resulting in the loss of both the DNS and ANS Systems entirely.

The main purpose of this chapter has been to illustrate the components of the ASL name sign system and the formation of the two distinct name sign types. Hopefully, this has helped to create a greater awareness of and sensitivity toward the traditional name signs used in the Deaf community. However, even if a name sign is formed in the traditional way, this does not mean that it will be used accordingly. Formation and use of name signs are two different things.

CHAPTER THREE

HOW TO USE
A NAME SIGN

THIS CHAPTER INTRODUCES THE READER to the traditional use and value of ASL name signs. In addition, the assignment of name signs and the choice between Descriptive and Arbitrary types will be discussed. Finally, the use of name signs in regular conversations will be addressed.

Historically, the ASL Name Sign System was used exclusively among Deaf people. Hearing people did not possess name signs because there was no reason for them to have one. Some exceptions include hearing teachers of the deaf whose students would assign them a name sign, as well as those hearing children born to Deaf parents. The times have now changed, and we have seen a dramatic increase in the number of hearing people learning ASL as a second or foreign language. Many of these hearing people have become friends with Deaf people, intermarry Deaf people, or work closely with Deaf people in certain professions (e.g., interpreting). Hearing parents of deaf children are among the newest group to come into contact with ASL, and more and more hearing people are entering the Deaf community in one way or another. Name signs have therefore become essential for hearing members of the Deaf community.

A name sign is of great value to a Deaf person because, without it, this person would have no effective means for identifying himself\herself or others. As discussed earlier, a name sign is a natural sign form. While its basic function is to identify a person, it also serves other important roles. Possessing a name sign actually marks a Deaf person's membership in the Deaf community. Thus, when a person is assigned a name sign, it can be seen "...as a kind of rite de passage, defining this entrance to the community through the bestowing of a name that is signed in the language of the (Deaf) subculture"(p. 239).[17] Recall the story of how I assigned name signs to my peers at school. I was one of the few native signers in the dormitory, and my peers looked to me to give them a name sign. Although I was only six years old at that time, I saw the need for their name signs. I wanted to refer to them when they were not present as they referred to me with my name sign. Deaf people recognize each other as part of a community, and this sense of community is firmly established with name signs.

I should emphasize again that some Deaf people simply do not have any name sign, but rather a fingerspelled name. As discussed earlier, this occurs mostly with those who have a short (English) name, and this does not mean that they are not members of the Deaf community. They are simply considered the exceptions. According to my observations, possessing a name sign is the norm in the Deaf community as it is also the norm for Deaf people to be assigned a name sign by somebody else. Sometimes, the role of assigning name signs is given to an authority figure in the Deaf community.[18] I assigned name signs most frequently at the elementary school level, where most deaf children find each other for the first time. Typically, they do not have a name sign if they come from a hearing family. Statistically, most deaf children are born to hearing parents, making up approximately 90 percent of the total population. Deaf children born to one or two Deaf parents (including myself) are a minority, approximately 10 percent.[19] A deaf child born to hearing parents most likely will not be assigned a name sign at birth. This denial of a name sign is often prolonged by the unfavorable policy toward ASL as a language of instruction in schools across the country.

This phenomenon has created some striking and unusual features involving how Deaf persons are assigned a name sign. According to one study, nearly one half of the Deaf adults were assigned a name sign as youngsters by peer group members. Only 42 percent received a name sign before the age of 5, whereas the remaining subjects received a name sign between the ages of 11 and 15.[20] These results are consistent with my own childhood experiences of assigning name signs to many of my peers. Again, the reason I was chosen to assign name signs was due to my background from a Deaf family.

Both descriptive name signs and arbitrary name signs are considered to be the primary names for Deaf people. However, the ANS System is considered the native name sign system due to its preference and use among Deaf parents. Therefore, when a child is born to Deaf parents, he or she will most likely receive an ANS as opposed to a DNS. It seems that Deaf parents dislike the idea of naming a child based on personal/physical characteristics.[21] DNSes are more popular in use among deaf children when they assign a name sign. When I was young, I assigned my peers either a DNS or ANS. However, as a parent naming my child, I have used the ANS System exclusively.

There is one explanation for the DNSes' popularity among deaf children, even though Deaf parents prefer ANSes. Unlike adults, deaf children tend to focus on other children's physical traits, and this may account for their preference of the DNS System.[22] This behavior is something that children, in general, lean towards as evidenced by nicknames they give to each other worldwide.[23] It is my belief that if all deaf children had Deaf parents, they would more likely receive an ANS at birth, and the role of DNSes would be different, most likely limited to that of a nickname. The lack of adult models that many Deaf people experienced in their childhood may have had an effect on the present role of the DNS and ANS Systems.

Non-traditional name signs, on the other hand, are a more recent trend, and I have observed that a number of deaf children now possess such name signs. One may suggest that there is a link between the rise in novice signing adults in the environment of deaf childrent. However, there is a number of schools and programs for deaf students that have considered accepting ASL as the language of instruction; thus, more

17

attention will be given to name signs. Deaf teachers and houseparents in these schools will be more desirable, and their presence in the deaf children's environment will create an impact, as will hopefully the publication of this book. With a better understanding of name signs in general, the ANS System is expected to become more popular than ever.

In assigning name signs to their children, Deaf and hearing parents need to make a choice between the ANS and DNS Systems. If an ANS is favored, they should keep in mind that a single location can be "reserved" for multiple name signs. Recall that my name sign and those of my brothers share the same chin location. It is a common practice among Deaf parents to have their children's name signs share the same location to represent the notion of family unity. Interestingly, the shared location for the family name sign is often limited to children and not their parents. For example, the location of my parents' name signs is different than mine or my brothers'; theirs are not on the chin. Thus, the shared location for name signs may best be described as a symbol for sibling unity.[24] The shared location for siblings is, of course, not required for every family, but is an option which deserves special mention.

The notion of a hearing person possessing a name sign is a much more complex issue. This is especially relevant when considering that the mere possession of a name sign symbolizes membership in the Deaf community. Thus, it is necessary for a hearing person to understand the true value of name signs according to the traditions of the Deaf community. An important first step is knowing the motivation behind a hearing person wanting a name sign. For example, if a hearing person is a college student taking ASL solely to fulfill a foreign language requirement, then the motivation may not be the same as for those who want to be involved with Deaf people in another capacity (e.g., to work with Deaf people or because they have a personal relationship with a Deaf person). The mere possession of a name sign indicates inclusion in the Deaf community. Thus, if a hearing person possesses a name sign just "for the fun of it," this indicates a disregard for the true value behind the name sign since the name sign serves no purpose or function in relation to the Deaf community.

Once a name sign is assigned to a hearing person, it can be changed only under specific circumstances. This is also true for a Deaf person. Basically, a name sign is expected to represent the identity of the person for the rest of his or her life. However, the name sign can be changed if social conditions require it. According to one study, if someone moves into a town and finds a person living there with an identical name sign, the newcomer is expected to change his or her name sign. It is also common for the elder or the person who has had the name sign for the longest to keep the name sign. If a Deaf person and a hearing person possess the same name sign, the hearing person would be expected to change his or her name sign.[25] This can be done by modifying or replacing it with a completely new name sign. The common approach is to modify the existing name sign as part of the **ASL Name Sign Modification System.**[26] Therefore, the existing name sign would be modified by adding an additional handshape. For example, a Deaf person may have the name Kathy and an ANS with a /**K**/ handshape. Suppose a hearing person whose name is "Kristy Williams" moves into town and also has the same name sign. It would be Kristy (the hearing person) who would need to modify her name sign. The name sign could be modified with the addition of a /**W**/ handshape (based on the initial of her last name). The original and modified name signs are illustrated below:

**Original Arbitrary
Name Sign**

Modified Arbitrary Name Sign

Following the assignment of a name sign, a person is expected to know how to use his or her name sign in a typical conversation. It is well known that English names can be used in a conversation in specific ways. For example, in a regular conversation, one can use a name to get someone's attention (e.g. "Hey, Mike"); for emphasis ("Mike, I cannot believe you."); and to refer to someone who is not present (e.g., "Can you tell Mike?") In comparison to English, ASL name signs are used only for the third example; thus name signs are used only to refer to a third person who is not present. For example, I would use a name sign in my conversation only if I am talking about a person other than the listener and myself. It is not proper for me to use my listener's name sign in a greeting. In order to greet my acquaintance, I simply sign "Hello" or, to get this person's attention, I wave my hand. Thus, there are distinct cultural patterns for using a name sign in a conversation.

When a formal introduction needs to be made between two persons, fingerspelling a name plays a vital role, and name signs are introduced later. Therefore, if I were to meet another Deaf person for the first time, I would introduce myself by fingerspelling my first and last names, usually without the use of my name sign. After we get to know each other, this new person would learn my name sign through a third party and begin using it thereafter.

This chapter has covered name sign assignment and how name signs are used. It has also stressed that ASL name signs possess special value and should be used accordingly. Both traditional formation and use of ASL name signs are now better understood through recent research.

CHAPTER FOUR

ORIGINS OF
NAME SIGNS

THIS CHAPTER INTRODUCES THE READER to the origination of name signs. The focus here is on the Deaf community and its contribution to the development of name signs. The Arbitrary Name Sign System's development and rise to become the dominant name sign type in the United States will also be discussed.

Proper names are important in a community; they provide a means for people to communicate amongst each other. The special relationship between proper names and community holds true for name signs and the Deaf community. This reciprocal relationship between naming and a sense of community has been illuminated by a number of research studies. One notable example is found on Providence Island in the Caribbean, where a large number of deaf people currently reside. Both deaf and hearing islanders are found communicating with each other in their own signed language; however, there is no true sense of a Deaf community on this island. It is reported that deaf islanders are isolated from each other and live unmarried by themselves scattered across the island. Although they are able to sign for communication with hearing people, they do not possess name signs.[27] Another case was found in China where deaf children were isolated from each other and did not have any name signs.[28] However, after making contact among themselves (e.g., in the school for the deaf), these Chinese children created their own name signs.[29]

Additional evidence comes from my own ongoing work with one Navajo clan which has several Deaf members; these Deaf Navajos possess a signed language (related to the Old Indian Sign Language) to communicate with each other and with all hearing clan members. The Deaf members never attended a school for the deaf, but, nevertheless, they have name signs which are descriptive in nature. It is quite remarkable that once deaf children are put together, there is a kind of magic that sparks the development and use of name signs. Apparently, a name sign will "...exist only in a group that consists of more than one deaf person." (p. 305)[30] Therefore, a name sign does not serve only as the identity of a person, but also indicates the existence of a Deaf community.

The earliest known Deaf community in the United States dates back to the 1700's, when a large population of Deaf people lived on Martha's Vineyard off the coast of Massachusetts.[31] Although signed language was widely used (by both Deaf and hearing islanders), there are no known records or documents of name signs on Martha's Vineyard. Unfortunately, there is no longer a sizable Deaf community on the island, and most of the hearing islanders no longer know nor use any signed language.

The social situation for Deaf people on Martha's Vineyard was ideal since they had extensive contact with each other, often married each other, and lived a very normal life.[32] The true sense of Deaf community seems to have existed there; thus, the likelihood of Deaf islanders having name signs is very high. Even though the ANS System is the dominant type of name sign used by Deaf people in the United States at present, we are not sure whether the ANS System originated on Martha's Vineyard. The historical record suggests that it did not. The handshapes used in the ANS System are strictly alphabetical; and the manual alphabet (as a system) did not reach the United States until the next century.

The manual alphabet originated in Spain in 1620 and was passed on to the United States in the early 1800's with the introduction of deaf education.[33] The founding of America's first permanent school for the deaf took place in Hartford, Connecticut in 1817 when Laurent Clerc, the school's first Deaf teacher, arrived from France, bringing with him both the manual alphabet and French Sign Language (FSL) to this country.[34] Interestingly, the largest group of students enrolled in the deaf school during that time were from Martha's Vineyard, and they brought their own signed language into the school which had an impact on the development of ASL.[35] There is no evidence that their name signs made any impact on the modern ANS System.

Assuming the ANS System did not originate on Martha's Vineyard, then the next question is whether the ANS System originated in France, with Clerc transplanting it to this country. Again, this does not seem to be the case. One piece of evidence to support this claim lies in the actual name signs used for prominent French people (both Deaf and hearing) in the eighteenth and nineteenth centuries. In America, name signs have historically been given to hearing people who were educators of the deaf, and this is also true for hearing educators in France. Abbé Charles-Michel de l'Epée was a hearing educator who founded the world's first public school for the deaf in Paris in 1755.[36] His name sign was not an ANS at all, but rather a DNS. Epée's own name sign was made up of two units; the first represents the shape of a priest's old-fashioned clerical collar located on the chest and the second unit is the sign for "sword," which is the English translation of his last name. The following page shows the illustration of his name sign.

I need to emphasize that the French DNS example above is not a possible DNS in ASL since it is made up of two units and since a DNS based on the meaning of an English name is not acceptable in ASL. Apparently, rules of formation for DNSes in ASL and FSL are different. However, DNSes were the type of name signs used for French people, including Epée's successors, Abbé Roch-Ambroise Sicard, and Roch-Ambroise Bebian. The prominent Deaf French educators and leaders of the Deaf community of that time, Jean Massieu, Ferdinand Berthier, and finally Clerc himself, also possessed DNSes.[37]

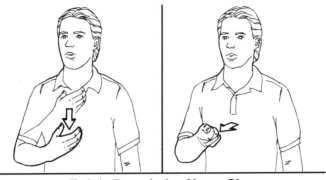

Epée's Descriptive Name Sign

Abbe Charles Michel de l'Epée

The following illustration of Clerc's DNS, depicting the scar on his cheek, was used in both France and the United States:[38]

Clerc's Descriptive Name Sign

American School for the Deaf

Laurent Clerc

Thomas Hopkins Gallaudet was the notable hearing American who brought Clerc to America to found the American School for the Deaf in Hartford. Gallaudet first spent considerable time in Paris studying the French method of instruction for deaf children. His name sign was also a DNS, presumably given to him by Deaf French people. We still use this same DNS to refer to him and for Gallaudet University in Washington, D.C., named in his honor.

The following illustration is Gallaudet's name sign which represents the glasses he wore:[39]

**T.H. Gallaudet's
Descriptive Name Sign**

Thomas Hopkins Gallaudet

Gallaudet University Archives

Up to this point, it seems clear that the ANS System did not exist in France during the time when its influence on the United States was most significant. Although there is no question that French Sign Language is the "mother language" of ASL,[40] it seems strange that the influence of French DNSes was not significant. It appears that the development of ASL name signs must have taken place after 1817; and, more specifically, the ANS System appears to have originated in the United States.

Finding the exact year in which the ANS System first appeared is quite difficult, since there was and still is no formal writing system for ASL. Because of this, the potential for recording Deaf people's name signs in ASL is virtually non-existent. However, I recently discovered an old record of name signs written in English at the Gallaudet University Archives.[41] This documentation of name signs, which describes specific forms, serves as our earliest record of the evolution of the ANS in ASL. Large volumes of records were made for students enrolled at the Pennsylvania School for the Deaf in Philadelphia dating back to the 1820's. Although not typical of most schools, each student had a record containing all relevant information, including his or her name sign. Fortunately, the records of these name signs are clear enough to enable us to recreate most of them.

Many of the name signs recorded are ANSes, thus confirming their use as early as the 1820's. One descriptive ANS example of a deaf student enrolled in the Pennsylvania school in 1833 is reprinted with the closest corresponding modern ANS as follows:

Gallaudet University Archives
1833 Arbitrary Name Sign

**Modern Arbitrary
Name Sign**

In addition, old photographs later taken of deaf students at the Pennsylvania School for the Deaf were also found. Not only do these photographs below reveal the faces of a student body, but they represent a wealth for more name sign data research.

Female Students at Pennsylvania School for the Deaf (1890's)

Gallaudet University Archives

Male Students at Pennsylvania School for the Deaf (1890's)

Although the evidence from the Pennsylvania School for the Deaf records reveals that the ANS System is at least 170 years old, this information does not reveal where the ANS System originated. In hopes of finding some answers, I asked the archivist at the American School for the Deaf in Hartford for the name sign of its very first and most famous deaf student, Alice Cogswell. He reported that her name sign is not known; it has apparently been lost.[42] At Gallaudet University, there is one building named in honor of Alice Cogswell, and many people have believed that the sign for this building is actually Alice's name sign. Unfortunately, this is not the case since the sign for Cogswell Hall is actually based on the sign for another building named after Walter Krug, a long-time Gallaudet professor.[43] Because the two buildings are identical, Krug's ANS was modified from a /K/ to a /C/ to represent Cogswell Hall.

Unfortunately, the name sign for another early Hartford student, Sophia Fowler, has also been lost. Although Fowler Hall at Gallaudet University was named after her, it has no sign. It is simply fingerspelled in abbreviation as /F-H/. Sophia is also an important figure in Deaf history. She and Alice Cogswell grew up together at the Hartford school, and Sophia married Thomas Hopkins Gallaudet (whose DNS was illustrated earlier). In 1837, they had a son, Edward Miner,[44] who later went on to found Gallaudet University. It is interesting to note that Edward Miner's name sign is now an ANS, different in type from his own father's. The ANS for Edward Miner Gallaudet is as follows:

E. M. Gallaudet's
Arbitrary Name Sign

Edward Miner Gallaudet

Gallaudet University Archives

Edward Miner Gallaudet became the first president of Gallaudet University, and the ANS tradition has been maintained by five presidents who followed him including the current president, I. King Jordan.[45] However, there are two exceptions to note: one is Dr. Elisabeth Zinser, who was forced to resign from the presidency following the infamous student protest in March 1988. Dr. Zinser was appointed president without possessing a name sign, indicating that she had never established any relationship with the Deaf community. The second exception is Dr. Jerry Lee, another president without a name sign. Because his last name was short, it was fingerspelled instead. All other presidents have possessed an ANS.[46]

In the early 1800's, Laurent Clerc married a Deaf woman named Eliza Boardman, and they had a daughter named Elizabeth.[47] In the portrait below painted in 1822, Ms. Clerc appears to be signing the name sign for her daughter.

Eliza Clerc and Daughter, Elizabeth

The handshape is an /E/ for the initial of the daughter's first name, and if, in fact, it is a true ANS, it would be classified as an ANS located in the neutral space with its movement shifting back and forth. Recall the earlier discussion on ANS types, Elizabeth's is an ANS in Neutral Space.[48] Edward Miner Gallaudet's ANS, on the other hand, is one of the Dual Locations on Body type. There is another portrait made earlier of Mr. Clerc himself when he was in France, and he was signing a /C/ handshape in front of his chest. This time, he is referring to the initial of his last written name. Although we are aware of the fact that Mr. Clerc possessed a DNS, the two aforementioned portraits indicate his association of the manual alphabet with the initial of written names. It appears that Mr. Clerc may have been the person who originated the idea of associating a name sign with written names, thus paving the way for further development of the ANS System.

The ANS for Elizabeth Clerc appears to be the oldest recorded name sign found in the United States. It is noted that the name signs for Clerc's and Gallaudet's children are ANSes, not DNSes, even though both Clerc and Gallaudet possessed DNSes. One possible explanation for their choice of ANSes in naming their children is that they both were involved in so-called language planning regarding the role of signing, and they were promoting the English version of Epée's Methodical Sign.[49] Initialization of signs was an approach which changed the handshape of a sign to that of the manual alphabet to conform to the initial of a written French or English word. Although, in both France and the United States, Methodical Sign was soon abandoned due to its ineffectiveness as a sign system,[50] many of the modern ASL signs remain initialized from that time. More recently, ASL signs have been subject to a further initialization process through the introduction of Manually Coded English, the modern version of Methodical Sign. Through initialized signs, alphabetical handshapes have been accepted as a part of ASL, and it appears that they have found their place in ASL, thus making the ANS System possible.[51]

The most interesting aspect of language planning is that when initialization of signs was first introduced in France, it was limited to regular signs. Recall that the name signs for prominent French people back in the eighteenth and nineteenth centuries were all DNSes, but many American name signs were ANSes. It appears that the model of initializing a sign was first borrowed from France and used in the United States with ASL. The difference with the American model, however, is that initialization was extended and used with name signs as well.

I should emphasize that initialized signs and ANSes are not

necessarily the same. It is true that alphabetical handshapes are used in both, but with initialized signs, a sign exists in its original form and undergoes an initialization process. For example, the original ASL sign, WATER, was probably similar to DRINK with the classifier handshape, /C/ indicating the shape of or way of holding a cup. With initialization, this classifier handshape is replaced with a /W/ to represent the initial of "water." The modified form of DRINK becomes the sign for WATER. Assuming this is the modification process that occurred, WATER is considered an initialized sign. In contrast, my name sign is not based on any existing ASL sign, thus it does not belong to the category of initialized signs.[52]

It is very possible that Clerc with Gallaudet introduced the ANS System upon the founding of their school, since their own children had ANSes. It appears that their motivation was to create and use name signs that were arbitrary in nature. The alphabetical handshapes were probably found to be less semantically significant as compared to classifier handshapes. The locations and movements for an arbitrary name sign system should also be the least semantically significant; certain locations and movements would be avoided since they possess significant meaning. For example, the mouth location provides meanings associated with the mouth itself and has become the location for the DNS, BUCKTEETH. In contrast, a location on the side of the chin (as used for my name sign) is far less semantically significant and has become one possible location for ANSes. Apparently, an evolutionary process initiated by Clerc occurred with the ANS System by creating specific locations and movement with reliance on alphabetical handshapes. This process seems to have resulted in the development of the ANS System as a subsystem of ASL.[53]

When the ANS System was first developed at the American School for the Deaf, it was brought to other schools for use as well. It is interesting to note that Clerc was on "loan" to the Pennsylvania School for the Deaf (PSD) after it was founded and was acting as its principal for seven months in 1821.[54] This brief stint at PSD coincides with the student records (discussed earlier) that included ANSes for many students. It seems plausible that Clerc brought his "new" name sign system from one school to another.

We have traced my own name sign back to the first few years of American deaf education. My parents did not have Deaf parents and therefore were not assigned name signs at birth. Yet, when they enrolled in residential schools for the deaf in the 1930's, they were assigned the ANSes that they now have. My father was enrolled in the South Dakota School for the Deaf in Sioux Falls, and my mother in the Washington School for the Deaf. Despite the different geographical locations of these schools, my parents share the same name sign type. Moreover, these schools are far west of the American and Pennsylvania schools where the ANS System first evolved. All evidence indicates that the ANS System, once developed, spread rapidly across the United States.

For whatever reason, the traditional name signs of France seem to have been abandoned and replaced with the ANS System around 1817, the year the American School for the Deaf was founded. In its process of evolution and development, the ANS System has become the dominant type used in the United States, yet a remaining area of interest pertains to why and how. This is especially relevant since Methodical Sign was also introduced to deaf children for use, but, unlike the ANS System, it did not succeed. It seems that the success of the ANS System may lie in its effectiveness as a system in terms of efficiency and meeting the needs of the Deaf community.

Efficiency is an important concept here since ANSes are comparable to regular signs and differ from a fingerspelled name. For example, the /S/ handshape of my own name sign is an accepted handshape in ASL since there are regular signs that have the same handshape (e.g., EXAGGERATE). The movement and locations of my name sign are also acceptable in ASL. The locations on both sides of the chin are also used for regular signs (e.g., BEARD). The singular path movement of my name sign also appears in many regular signs (e.g., DEAF). Thus, my name sign is as legitimate as any regular ASL sign.[55] A fingerspelled name, on the other hand, is strikingly different since it is not a sign and tends to be much less efficient.[56]

Other than efficiency, the value system that Deaf people have in regard to name signs may have an impact as well. As discussed earlier, American Deaf people appear to eschew naming their children based on personal/physical characteristics. By contrast, Deaf people in

Sweden have a different value system regarding name signs, and they seem to favor name signs that are descriptive in nature.[57] It is important to reiterate that, although DNSes may be based on a person's personal/physical characteristics, they are not necessarily bad or negative. A DNS can be positive in reference to a person, and it can be seen as more "personalizing" than an ANS. This positive perspective of DNSes may be what the Swedish Deaf community has adopted. Yet, here in the United States, the value system has been in favor of name signs that are arbitrary in nature, thus causing the ANS type to be perceived as "better" or "more appropriate." The dominance of the ANS System is clearly made possible by its support and encouragement from the American Deaf people's value system.

Assuming the ANS System originated in the United States, it is still important to understand that the ANS System has its roots in France, where the notion of initializing signs originated and in Spain, where the alphabetical handshapes were originated many years earlier. One should also understand that the ANS System's origin was not natural, but rather a product of language planning in the early years of American deaf education. Therefore, it appears that language planning can be successful if done properly and if it gains support from the Deaf community. It was the unique combination of Clerc's and Gallaudet's efforts, the efficiency of the system, and the value system of American Deaf people that led to the success of the ANS System.

I wonder what would have happened if the "intervention" of language planning did not take place; perhaps, the ANS System would not be what it is today. It would be interesting to see what the ANS System would look like if the Deaf community had developed it without using the manual alphabet. One may also wonder about the relationship of the ANS System and English. It is clear by now that the alphabetical handshape used in an ANS actually refers to the initial of a person's written name. Yet, one must remember that an ANS does not represent an entire written name; for example, with my own ANS, one would not know to which English proper name it refers (i.e., Steve, Seth, or any other name starting with a /S/). The fingerspelled counterpart of my written name, however, is far more representative of English than is my ANS. As discussed earlier, my ANS is as

35

legitimate as any sign in ASL, although I do not deny that it incorporates "limited" English representation. Regardless of what type of name signs are involved, either arbitrary or descriptive, or whether alphabetical handshapes are used, name signs do serve a definite and distinct function in the Deaf community as symbols for both the identification of a person and membership in a community.

In sum, the story of how I got my name sign indicates that my name sign is part of a long history dating back to approximately 1817 and of the development of the ANS System. The fact that, at the age of six, my brother Ted helped my parents select an ANS for me demonstrates that he had acquired knowledge of the name sign system. The same holds true for me when, at six years of age, I was also busy assigning name signs to my peers at school. My parents did not acquire the name sign knowledge from their hearing parents, but rather from their deaf peers who had Deaf parents. Similarly, I shared my knowledge of name signs with my peers (who happened to have hearing parents) by my examples in forming and using name signs. Throughout the years, deaf children have maintained this tradition by assigning name signs to one another. This phenomenon is indeed remarkable and accounts for how the ANS System has endured up to this day. An interesting parallel prevails here since ASL as a language has also been maintained in this fashion through many Deaf generations.[58]

Unfortunately, in recent years, the tradition of name signs has been subject to external influences as evidenced by the rising number of non-traditional name signs in both form and use. This phenomenon is perhaps due to mere ignorance of the name sign tradition. The goal of this book has been to preserve the name sign tradition according to the Deaf community. I have discussed in detail how name signs are formed and used and where they originated, in addition to providing a list of ANSes that can be chosen and used to help further preserve the name sign tradition. This name sign list is the first of its kind, made possible through my own research. It is hoped that the availability of ANSes in a reference format will enable more people to possess ANSes and share in the rich heritage of Deaf Americans.

ENDNOTES

1 S. S. Supalla, 1990.

2 T. Supalla, 1985.

3 Meadow, 1977. The identification of ANSes and DNSes from the data is the author's interpretation.

4 S. Supalla, 1990.

5 Meadow, 1977.

6 Battison, 1978.

7 S. Supalla, 1990.

8 Mindess, 1990.

9The /Z/ handshape is excluded because its obligatory internal movement of tracing the shape of the letter "Z" is a shape description rather than an arbitrary alphabetical symbol (S. Supalla, 1990). It should be added that /Z/ differs from another shape-based alphabetical handshape, /J/. /Z/ requires three different movements as compared to one for /J/, and, as a result, it would be awkward to repeat the movement of /Z/ as required for an ANS.

10 S. Supalla, 1990.

11The locations on the body are, in fact, more restricted as compared to those of regular signs; the same is true for the contacting regions of the hand. Movements are also more restricted; for example, a circular movement is not acceptable for an ANS. See S. Supalla (1990) for further discussion on the linguistic description of the ANS System.

12 Wilbur, 1979.

13 Mindess, 1990.

14 Smith, 1988.

15 Mindess, 1990.

16 Mindess, 1990.

17 Meadow, 1977.

18 Mindess, 1990.

19 Rainer, Altshuler, and Kallman, 1963; and Schein and Delk, 1974. The 90-percent versus 10-percent figure is likely to be an underestimate supported by data from the 1984-85 Annual Survey of Hearing Impaired Children and Youth (Jordan and Karchmer, 1986).

20 Meadow, 1977.

21 S. Supalla, 1990.

22 Mindess, 1990.

23 Morgan et al., 1979.

24 Meadow, 1977; Mindess, 1990; S. Supalla, 1990.

25 Mindess, 1990.

26 S. Supalla, 1990.

27 Washabaugh, 1980; 1986.

28 Yau, 1985.

29 Yau et al., 1989.

30 Yau et al., 1989.

31 Groce, 1985.

32 Groce, 1985.

33 Moores, 1978.

34 Moores, 1978; Woodward, 1978; Lane, 1984.

35 Groce, 1985.

36 Lane, 1984.

37 Personal communication with Guy Bouchauveau (October 1990).

38 Hotchkiss, 1913.

39 Stokoe et al., 1965.

40 Woodward, 1978.

41 Special thanks to Michael Olson for pointing out the existence of such records.

42 Personal communication with Loy Golladay (August 1990).

43 Personal communication with Carol Padden and Gil Eastman (September 1990).

44 Lane, 1984.

45 Dr. I. King Jordan's name sign may be an ANS, but it is also a homophone with a lexical sign in ASL: KING.

46 Personal communication with Clayton Valli (January 1991).

47 Lane, 1984.

48 Elizabeth Clerc's name sign is also believed to be an /E/, but its location is on the shoulder/heart area; personal communication with Loy Golladay (August 1990). Both name signs are still ANSes.

49 Lane, 1984.

50 Lane, 1980.

51 S. Supalla, 1990.

52 S. Supalla, 1990.

53 S. Supalla, 1990.

54 Gannon, 1981.

55 S. Supalla, 1990.

56 See S. Supalla (1990) for further discussion on the relationship of ANSes with ASL and English.

57 Hedberg, 1989.

58 Meadow, 1972.

PART TWO

THE NAME
SIGN LIST

CHOOSING A NAME SIGN

THE PURPOSE OF THE NAME SIGN LIST is to provide the reader with a wide selection of ASL name signs. The list is comprised of a collection of 525 name signs, all of which are the Arbitrary Name Sign (ANS) type. They do not have any inherent meaning other than as name signs.

The first step in selecting a name sign is choosing the manual alphabet letter that corresponds to the initial of one's first, middle, or last (English) name. For example, if a reader has the first name, Bill, he can refer to the /B/ category in the list where there is a total of 20 /B/ name signs available from which to choose. Please remember that one should not choose a name sign without consulting with the local Deaf community since there should not be any two persons sharing an identical name sign. This would only defeat the purpose of having a name sign.

Most readers will be faced with a wide selection of name signs in each letter category, so one should be aware that one name sign may be more appropriate for him or her than another. Some people believe that certain name signs are associated with gender. For example, the chin location tends to be reserved for female name signs, whereas the forehead or temple location is reserved for male name signs. However, according to my ongoing research, it seems that there is insufficient data to support this claim. My research does identify certain name signs that appear to be more formal than others. For example, ANSes with one location on the body are considered more plain, equivalent to "Joe" or "Jane." In contrast, ANSes with dual locations on the body are considered more fancy, equivalent to "Richard" or "Jacqueline." Further research is needed for more accurate information regarding the significance of locations and movement for name signs.

If the reader likes a particular name sign that is used for someone in the local Deaf community, it can always be modified by adding one more letter from the manual alphabet. The second letter should refer to the initial of the reader's middle or last name. That is, if the last name begins with a /K/, the handshape should be a /K/. In the example of "Bill" above, the result would be a /BK/ ANS. By adding one more letter to an existing name sign, the total of possible ANSes increases from hundreds to thousands.

The reader should be aware that an ANS may coincide in form with an ASL sign (e.g., a /C/ on the heart/shoulder is also POLICE). In this case, the homophone of an ANS and an ASL sign prevails and should be avoided since an ANS should not retain any inherent meaning. In accordance, a small number of ANSes that are identical to ASL signs have been removed from the following name sign list.

Finally, if the reader prefers a name sign that has inherent meaning based on personal characteristics, he or she will not find one on this list. Again, the Descriptive Name Sign is a completely different type of ASL name sign. As discussed throughout this book, according to the traditions of the Deaf community, the ANS type is considered the preferred type of name sign in the United States. If the reader wishes to be sensitive towards the values of Deaf people, this fact must be considered when selecting a name sign.

It is truly hoped that your new understanding of name signs and the American Deaf community will add to your enjoyment in making your selection of an Arbitrary Name Sign.

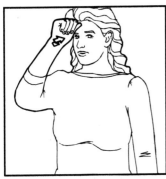

CHOOSING A NAME SIGN

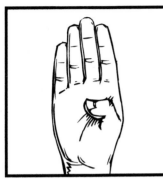

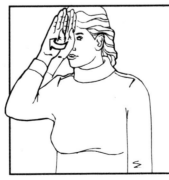

CHOOSING A NAME SIGN

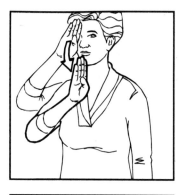  

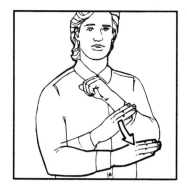 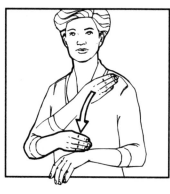 

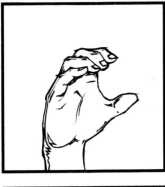

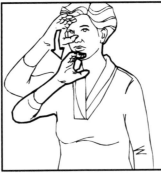

CHOOSING A NAME SIGN

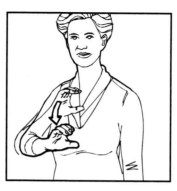
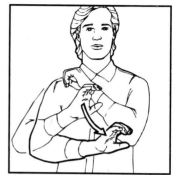

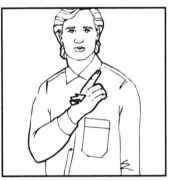

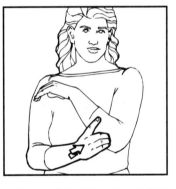

CHOOSING A NAME SIGN

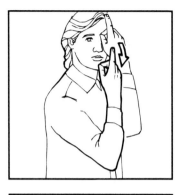  

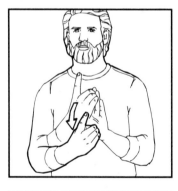  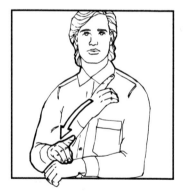

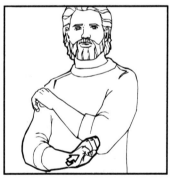

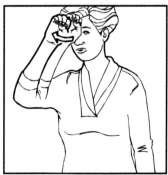

CHOOSING A NAME SIGN

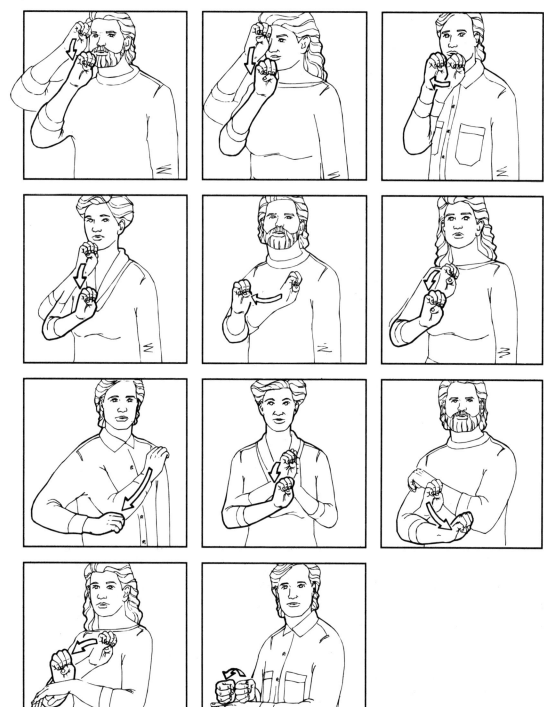

53

CHOOSING A NAME SIGN

  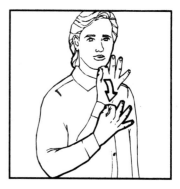

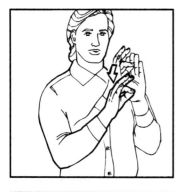 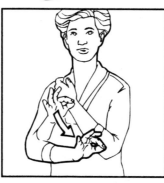 

55

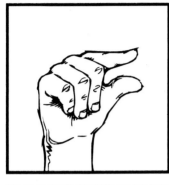

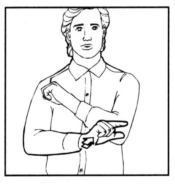

CHOOSING A NAME SIGN

CHOOSING A NAME SIGN

CHOOSING A NAME SIGN

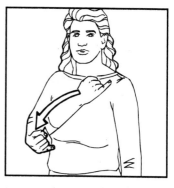

CHOOSING A NAME SIGN

The movement is strictly "brushing" for all /J/ ANSes.

63

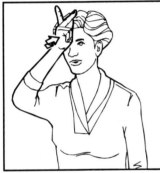

CHOOSING A NAME SIGN

THE BOOK OF
NAME SIGNS

CHOOSING A NAME SIGN

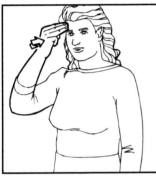

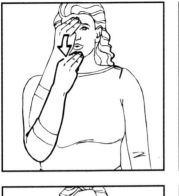

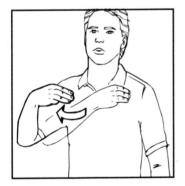

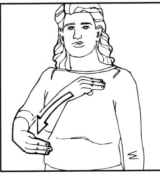

CHOOSING A NAME SIGN

 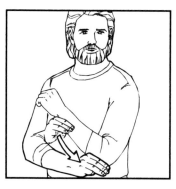 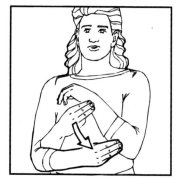

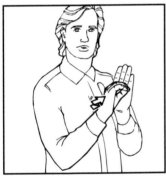

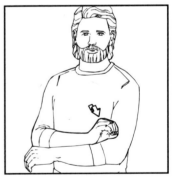

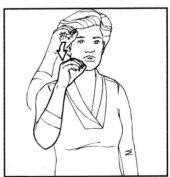

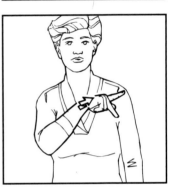

CHOOSING A NAME SIGN

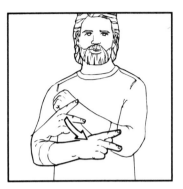

CHOOSING A NAME SIGN

79

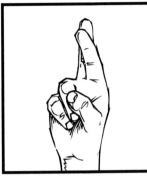

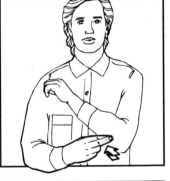

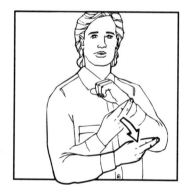
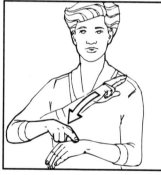

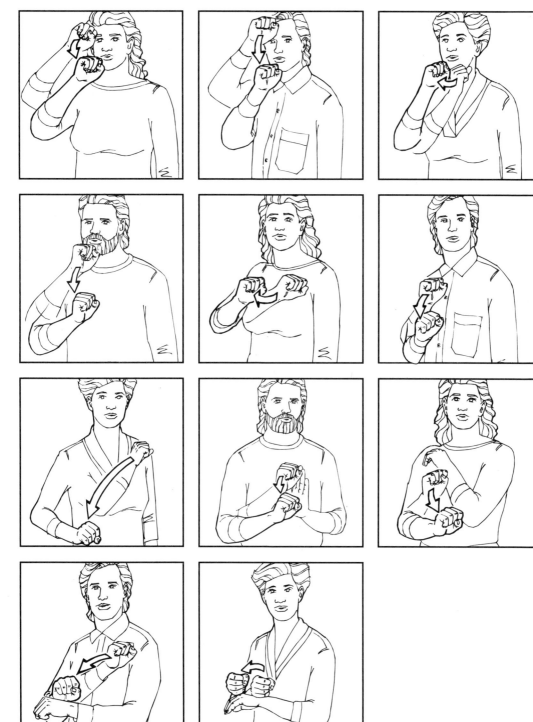

CHOOSING A NAME SIGN

  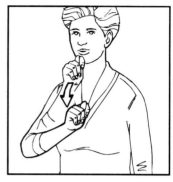

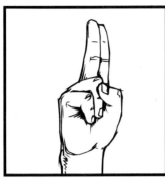

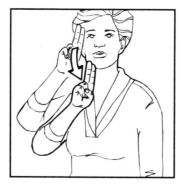

CHOOSING A NAME SIGN

THE BOOK OF
NAME SIGNS

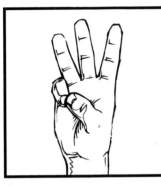  

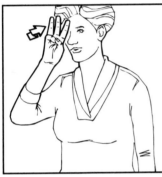  

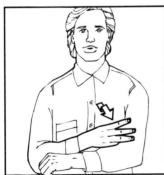  

90

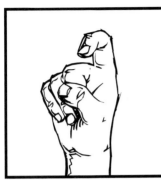

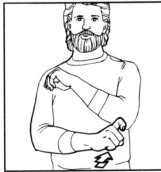

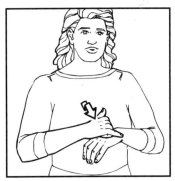

LIST OF REFERENCES

Battison, R. 1978. Lexical Borrowing in American Sign Language. Silver Spring, MD: Linstok Press.

Gannon, J. 1981. Deaf Heritage. Silver Spring, MD: National Association of the Deaf.

Groce, N. 1985. Everyone Here Spoke Sign Language: A Hereditary Deafness on Martha's Vineyard. Cambridge, MA: Harvard University Press.

Hotchkiss, J. 1913. Memories of Old Hartford. (Video) Washington, DC: Gallaudet University.

Hedberg, T. 1989. Name Signs in Swedish Sign Language: Their Formation and Use. Paper presented at the Deaf Way Conference. Washington, DC: Gallaudet University.

Jordan, I. & M. Karchmer. 1986. Patterns of Sign Use Among Hearing Impaired Students. In A. Schildrot and M. Karchmer (Eds.), *Deaf Children in America*. San Diego, CA: College-Hill Press.

Lane, H. 1980. Historical: A Chronology of the Oppression of Sign Language in France and the United States. In H. Lane & F. Grosjean (Eds.), *Recent Perspectives on American Sign Language*. Hillsdale, NJ: Lawrence Erlbaum

Lane, H. 1984. When the Mind Hears: A History of the Deaf. New York, NY: Random House.

Meadow, K. 1972. Sociolinguistics, Sign Language, and the Deaf Culture. In T. O'Rourke (Ed.), *Psycholinguistics and Total Communication: The State of the Art.* Washington, DC: American Annals of the Deaf.

Meadow, K. 1977. Name Signs as Identity Symbols in the Deaf Community. *Sign Language Studies.* 16: 237-246. Silver Spring, MD: Linstok Press.

Mindess, A. 1990. What Name Signs Can Tell Us About Deaf Culture. *Sign Language Studies.* 66:1-24. Silver Spring, MD: Linstok Press.

Moores, D. 1978. Educating the Deaf: Psychology, Principles, and Practices. Boston, MA: Houghton Mifflin.

Morgan, J. , C. O. Neill, & R. Harre. 1979. Nicknames: Their Origins and Social Consequences. London, England: Routledge and Kegan Paul.

Rainer, J., K. Altshuler, & F. Kallman. 1963. Family and Mental Health Problem in a Deaf Population. New York, NY: New York State Psychiatric Institute.

Smith, C. 1988. Signing Naturally: Notes on the Development of the ASL Curriculum Project at Vista College. *Sign Language Studies*. 59:171-182. Silver Spring, MD: Linstok Press

Schein , J. & M. Delk. 1974. The Deaf Population of the United States. Silver Spring, MD: National Association of the Deaf.

Stokoe, W., D. Casterline, & C. Croneberg. 1965. A Dictionary of American Sign Language on Linguistic Principles. Washington, DC: Gallaudet University Press.

Supalla, S. 1990. The Arbitrary Name Sign System in American Sign Language. *Sign Language Studies,* 67: 99-126. Silver Spring, MD: Linstok Press.

Supalla, T. 1985. The Classifier System in American Sign Language. In C. Craig (Ed.), *Noun Classification and Categorization*. Philadelphia, PA: Benjamin's North America.

Wilbur, R. 1979. American Sign Language and Sign Systems. Baltimore, MD: University Park Press.

Washabaugh, W. 1980. The Organization and Use of Providence Island Sign Language. *Sign Language Studies*. 26: 65-92. Silver Spring, MD: Linstok Press.

Washabaugh, W. 1986. Five Fingers for Survival. Ann Arbor, MI: Karoma.

Woodward, J. 1978. Historical Bases of American Sign Language. In P. Siple (Ed.), *Understanding Language through Sign Language Research*. New York, NY: Academic Press.

Yau, S. 1985. Sociological and Cognitive Factors in the Creation of a Sign Language by an Isolated Deaf Person Within a Hearing Community. In W. Stokoe & V. Volterra (Eds.), *Actes du III International Symposium on Sign Language Research*. Silver Spring, MD & Rome, Italy: Linstok Press & Instituto di Psicologia, CNR.

Yau, S., & He Jingxian. 1989. How Deaf Children in a Chinese School Get Their Name Signs. *Sign Language Studies*. 65: 305-322. Silver Spring, MD: Linstok Press.

ABOUT THE AUTHOR

Samuel J. Supalla is an Assistant Professor and the Director of Sign Language/Deaf Studies in the Department of Special Education and Rehabilitation at the University of Arizona in Tucson. He has done extensive research on Manually Coded English and its impact on language development of Deaf children. His research domain ranges from theoretical aspects of signed language development and language planning and policy issues, to ASL literature. Dr. Supalla is an accomplished filmmaker and ASL storyteller. Currently Dr. Supalla, his wife Robin, and son Ryan are anxiously awaiting ther new arrival and additional name sign to the family.